COLLEGE READY 101

A field guide to a successful freshman year

by Dedra Eatmon, Ph.D.

Table of Contents

Introduction

The struggle is real. Knowing what to do and staying motivated to do it can be a challenge for some of us. Many of us. Despite what you may think, grown-ups don't have it all together. Sometimes we struggle with staying on task, meeting deadlines, and keeping ourselves from falling down the rabbit hole of Instagram, Netflix or whatever our distraction of choice may be. The struggle only gets harder when we are adjusting to a new job, new school, or experiencing some other type of change in our lives. Let's be honest, when I say we, I mainly mean me. I share this with you because I want you to know that we all have to work at being (or staying) great. It doesn't happen on its own. And it's okay if you sometimes feel clueless about where to start and how to maintain. Grown-ups have been adulting for years and we still have to make an effort, so why wouldn't you?

Being a college student isn't always easy. In fact, being a college student can be hard. You probably know all the things to do to get there. Standardized tests . . . Check. Applications and essays submitted by the deadline . . . Check. You wait and then, acceptance . . . Check. The rest is a cake walk, right? Not exactly. It's like the tag line from that MTV show,

"You think you know, but you have no idea." Once your parents drop you off, college life begins for real. Unless you started undergrad before and left for your own reasons, being a college student - a freshman no less - is uncharted territory for most of you reading this book. You go in armed with all the things that worked for you in high school, but here's the kicker. No one tells you that being great in high school doesn't automatically translate to being a kick-ass college student. "Lies!" you say. Nope, it's true. While being a great high school student is a start, it takes a different set of skills and sensibilities to be a great college student. Don't worry, though. I have you covered.

College Ready 101 will help you make the shift from high school to college and do it well. It's not an end all, be all comprehensive list of everything you need to know to be a successful college student, but it will get you started. It also won't turn you into a kick-ass student, but it gives you specific action items to get on that path. By no means is everything you need to know between the covers of this guide because it would probably be much longer than you'd like. This book addresses many academic situations, but everything isn't about classes. There are residential, professional, and personal situations that are covered as well.

I thought about what would be most helpful for you as you start college. I also thought about the best way to deliver information to you. You're a college freshman whose day is filing up with activities and you may not want to dig through the pages of a book to get direction. You want small, easy to digest chunks, right? *College Ready 101* is full of bite-sized informational nuggets. I started to call it a quick-reference guide, but the reality is that I wrote this for you to get the knowledge while you are in the throws of navigating college life. This book is a field guide. Nothing more, nothing less. In fact, this introduction is probably the most number of consecutive sentences you'll see in the book. The goal is to make it easy for you. Thumb through, find your nugget, and go.

General College Life

Just a few tips for adjusting to your new environment.

1. College bound is not the same thing as college ready.

    a. Believe it or not, only approximately 40% of high school seniors are prepared for the academic demands and responsibilities of college (NCES, 2016).

       College readiness requires a set of traits and characteristics that are indirectly associated with grades and scores, curiosity and openness, creativity, accountability, humility, and character (Sullivan, 2012).

       It is also based on possessing and understanding four core components: key cognitive strategies, content knowledge, academic behaviors and, contextual skills and awareness (Conley, 2008).

       "The college ready student . . . is able to understand what is expected in a college course, can cope with content knowledge that is presented, and can develop key intellectual lessons and dispositions the course is designed to convey" (Conley, 2008). In other words, they not only have the academic background, but are prepared for the intellectual stretch that occurs in their new environment.

b. Whether you've been exposed to college life and expectations or not, adequately encouraged to develop these traits or not, you can get college ready now. Prepare for a journey of learning that will require you to open your mind, possibly shed parts of your old identity and receive the education and environment that surrounds you. In other words – get your life!

2. You don't know what you don't know.

a. One major reason to attend college is for personal intellectual growth. Go to college with a growth mindset. Not only does someone with a growth mindset recognize that they don't know everything, they are also more resilient and do not look at failure or set-backs as evidence that they aren't intellectually capable. A growth mindset is one that views "failures" as learning experiences and also views intellect as expandable. It's not an "either you know it or you don't" scenario. It's more like "I don't know/understand it *yet*, but I can." (Dweck, 2006).

b. Understand that you don't know everything pertaining to the next phase(s) of your life. If you did, you wouldn't be in college. Open your mind to learning new things about yourself, about your world view, about your abilities, etc.

3. Get comfortable with being uncomfortable.

    a. The way you live and learn is college is markedly different than anything you've experienced up to this point. Being open and curious apply here as well. College is one of the few times in your life when you will have a mixing pot of ideologies, backgrounds, music, culture, and lifestyle at your fingertips. Check out as much as you can, both inside and outside the classroom.

    b. Take an elective that may be something you wanted to try, but seems "weird" or "corny". If you're a STEM major, choose an arts/humanities elective. Social sciences? Try a coding course. If you're not ready to commit to a class, join a club.

4. In high school, smart students don't usually need help. In college, smart students SEEK it.

    a. In your former life (high school) you may not have needed much, if any, assistance when completing your work. Furthermore, teachers tend to look out for their strongest to prevent some challenges from even happening. As a college freshman, you are expected to have a sense of self-awareness that dictates you know how and when to use campus resources. The fact of the matter is that you may not have experienced difficulty in completing an assignment before, so how in the world can you be expected to process those feelings and then have the wherewithal to do something about it, right?

b. Ask for help as soon as you don't understand something. The earlier the better. Your professors and TAs are usually happy to help. (See #16.)

5. Use a planner – preferably paper, but your phone will do.

a. Time management is one of the biggest issues professors mention with first year students. By writing down each of your appointments, assignment due dates, and other big dates, you are better able to visualize how things are going and keep up with your schedule. This is probably the most foundational of all self-management and study skills (Conley, 2008).

b. Use a planner – digital or on paper. Doesn't matter which., Just use one. Once the *College Ready Student Planner* is complete you can order yours at tasseltotassel.com.

6. The quality of work you submitted in high school may not stack up to what is required of you as a college student.

a. So you were a great high school student. That's nice. Let that go. You are now a college student and graduating from high school does not automatically make you ready for college. (Remember the 40%?) You are going to be pushed to another level as a college student, so expect to work at least a little harder than you did in high school. You're in the majors now. Remember that scene in *Love & Basketball* where Monica was basking in the glow of her jump shot during practice while the rest of the team moved to the other end of the court? Don't be Monica. Level up.

b. Consider that you aren't as great a writer as you think you are, despite your high school grades. Again, you're not regurgitating and your professors expect you to improve and respond well to feedback. Always have someone review your writing before you submit it – your professor, the writing center, etc. This means you have to complete your paper/project 24-48 hours in advance to allow time for review. (You built in that buffer time using your planner, right?) Take this approach with all your major assignments for every course.

Academic, Inside the Classroom

Suggested behaviors and actions that you can employ in class that will set you up for success.

7. Going to class isn't optional.

    a. While you will read before class and lecture mostly fills in the gaps (see #13), going to class is the glue that holds all the intellectual and conceptual pieces together. There may be information shared in class that supplements the reading. Class discussions, and the resulting exchanges can be helpful in understanding your material.

    b. Go to class. Go To Class. GO TO CLASS! Every single one. Although many large classes do not take daily attendance, it is important to attend. Missing one day makes you more comfortable missing an additional day, and that is not a habit you want to create. Trust me, it does not end well. At some point you will miss too much work to catch up. You have also missed the opportunity to interact with your classmates (creating that support system) and to create a relationship with your instructor.

8. Showing up isn't enough.

    a. As a high school student, you may or may not have put forth full effort to do much in class. If you are particularly bright, you picked things up as your teacher explained them. Now that you're in college, however, there is much more to learning and being a good student. Since most of your learning will happen outside of class (see #13), it is imperative that you stay on top of that and use lecture/class time to your advantage. This includes getting to class – on time – sitting somewhere you can hear and see well, taking notes, and asking questions. While putting your bum in a seat is a good start, there is much more to being a good college student than showing up.

b. Be an active learner by being prepared for each class meeting, taking notes and asking questions.

9. There is a cognitive process that happens when handwriting your notes as opposed to typing them.

a. Using a laptop for note-taking allows you to capture more of what is shared during lecture verbatim, but that does not always translate into better understanding of the information that is being shared. Typed notes are equally as effective for recalling facts and figures but are not conducive to the conceptual application of your material (Mueller & Oppenheimer, 2016.). (Laptops can also easily be a source of distraction when lecture becomes less interesting, so keeping it closed isn't the worst idea).

b. Take notes in class. Handwrite them and draw figures, etc. when necessary. While I prefer to you take hand-written notes, I urge you to take them with whatever method works for you. (One well-known method is Cornell. A link to it and others are listed in Appendix A.)

10. Many teachers teach to the front of the room and this is where you want to be when in class.

a. In high school, your class size probably allowed the teacher to see everyone's face and/or walk around to monitor your progress. Many classes in college operate as lectures and your instructor isn't going to circulate around the classroom. They will stand at the front, share information, and take questions. In larger classrooms and lecture halls, they will often focus their attention on the students they can see easily - those who sit in the front. It's not intentional, it's just what happens. That means you want to sit up close, where the instructor can see your face and perhaps respond to any confusion they see on your face.

b. Sit as close to the front of the classroom as possible. If you cannot sit in the front 2 rows of a class/lecture, sit in the center. Imagine the letter T; the first two rows are the top of the T and the center of the room is the downstroke. Sit there.

Academic, Outside of Class

Useful information about things like when
and how to study, what resources are
available to help, and how to better
ease into the habit of studying.

11. Having a text book is also more important than you may think.

    a. While you may not read an ENTIRE text during the course of the semester, there will be information in it you need. Get access to one. If for some reason your instructor says you do not need it, check your syllabus to determine how much of the content you are expected to read, ask someone who's taken (and made a good grade) in the course whether that is true, and make sure there is one copy on reserve in the library.

    b. You NEED the text. Get (access to) the book(s) for your course. Purchase, rent, or borrow it from a friend or the library reserve.

12. The information in the text is for your intellectual growth and edification.

    a. Your textbooks aren't meant to level tables and/or serve as coasters. They are part of the course because the information in them is necessary as a foundation for a concept that will be taught or discussed. If you don't read the text but instead expect your instructor to give you every single detail, you will be highly disappointed in the college process. You are expected to read the assigned pages, understand what you've read, and to some extent summarize and apply it.

b. You must READ the text. Ideally, read the assigned section before class to get more out of your lecture.

13. The majority of learning in college, particularly freshman year, happens outside of class. Lecture is there to fill in the blanks, not to TEACH you a concept.

a. In college, you are expected to be an independent, self-reliant learner (Conley, 2008) who has deep thought about what is being presented.

b. Read the assigned text before class and re-read your notes after class. Ask questions during lecture to fill in the gap and/or reinforce what was learned.

14. The room where your class is held IS NOT your professor's office.

a. In college, your professor/instructor has an office and they teach in a space that is separate from the classroom (or conference/seminar room).

    b. Use the course syllabus (or class management system) to find out both where your class meets and where your professor's office is located.

15. Initiate a professional relationship your instructor sooner rather than later.

    a. In some instances, your college class may have hundreds of people. This large class size makes it difficult for your instructor (or TA) to get to know each student.

    b. Meet your professor during the first three weeks of class. Introduce yourself after class if possible. If not, go to your professor's office hours and introduce yourself. (A sample conversation starter is in Appendix B.)

16. Office hours are designated times where you see your professor to ask questions, get clarification, etc.

    a. Not enough students utilize office hours. They are designed to give you an opportunity to explore course material, develop relationships with your professor, and learn/experience how the academic system operates.

b. Go to see your professor/TA at least once per week, whether you feel you need assistance or not. This keeps you on top of every concept that is taught and helps you develop a relationship with your instructor. If you don't have questions, then go anyway and say hello. (We really do appreciate that.)

17. Instructors enjoy when you come to office hours in an effort to be better or learn more.

a. Part of being a successful college student lies in your ability to be resourceful and utilize what is available to you, despite the fact that you may have to seek it out now. Assistance from your professor/TA is one of those things. Office hours are an opportunity to get clarification about things that were unclear in your reading or lecture. They are also an opportunity to get assistance with concepts that present challenges to you.

b. When you see your professor, have questions that are related to a specific assignment, homework problem, or reading. "I don't understand any of this." (See Appendix C for sample verbiage.)

18. Instructors do not enjoy when you come to office hours to beg for a grade.

   a. On some level you know that college operates differently than high school, but on another level you have expectations that it will. Very rarely in college will you be given make-up work or extra credit. College is going to prepare you for your professional (and adult) life through both content and attitude. As a college student, there is a higher level of accountability. The consequences of your (in)action – whether that's missing an assignment, not putting forth full effort, or blowing it off – are ones you have to accept and move on. Instructors have hundreds of students and in some instances, you get what you get.

   b. Let's say you recognize and accept that perhaps you didn't do as much as you could to earn a grade on an assignment, quiz or test. When you do see your professor, be prepared to have a conversation owning up to the role you played in your current academic standing and ask what, if anything, can be done to improve your grade for the remainder of the course. It's also a great time to share what you do not understand and determine whether the prof or TA can give you some assistance in getting up to speed. With this, also be prepared for the instructor to not be as accommodating as your high school teachers may have been. Some will, but some will not. It's not personal, it's college.

19. Go to office hours with specific questions to ask.

    a. Office hours are designated times where you see your professor to ask questions, get clarification, etc. (See #16).

    b. Attend office hours at least ONCE per week from the beginning of the semester; at the very least when you are confused or your earned grade is less than goal (See Appendix C for sample verbiage).

20. Studying and doing homework *are not* the same thing.

    a. Study skills encompass activities that go beyond reading the text and answering the homework questions (Conley, 2008). You are no longer taking in information to regurgitate it for a quiz or test. You are expected to participate in an exchange of ideas and to solve problems with no clear solutions. You are expected to contribute to the academic discourse. Doing homework means attempting to answer the questions and/or solve the problems that are assigned. To put it more simply, let me quote my godson ... "Homework is completing problems that are due in the next day or so. Studying is reviewing material to make sure I understand."

b. Do your homework, but also study. It's a good idea to know your learning style (the most effective method for you to take in and process information) and incorporate that into how you study. At the very least, read the text, take notes, and make flash cards when/if you can. Writing down questions about confusing concepts also gives you something to ask in class or during office hours (See #9 and #16).

21. The general rule of thumb is to study two (2) hours outside of class for every hour (50-minute block) you are in class (e.g. a 3-credit hour class requires 6 hours of studying).

a. Faculty reports students need to spend at least two times more than what they currently spend preparing for class (NSSE, 2006).

b. Block off study time in your planner. If 2:1 seems like a lot at first, ease into it with 45 minutes, then 1 hour, etc.

22. Working with others can be helpful in cementing concepts and getting multiple perspectives on a single idea/concept.

    a. Being able to share and explain information with others verifies your understanding.

    b. Create study groups. (Hint: These may or may not be your friends.) If you already know others in your course, even from other sections, suggest that you study together. If not, pay attention to the students who ask good questions and ask to study with them. When in doubt, study up.

23. Study time should be dedicated to studying, not getting ready to study, finding your playlist, etc.

    a. Studying requires you to focus, without distraction. Setting up your playlists and sometimes listening to music or watching an episode of "grown-*ish*" can negatively impact how well you learn. High levels of multi-tasking have been associated with lower exam scores. The brain divides attention between tasks and the level of focus for a single task (studying) decreases when other tasks are incorporated. It also takes your brain up to 45 minutes to regain focus after interruptions and switched tasks (Patterson, 2017; Rekhart, 2012).

b. Reduce distractions by putting your phone on DND. No Netflix and no social media. After 45-minute blocks of studying, reward yourself by watching 5-10 min of YouTube, streaming, etc.

24. Shifting your study habits from high-school to college-level requires effort for most of us.

a. The facets of college readiness include academic behaviors (Conely, 2008). Your college instructors have different goals than your high school teachers. Through covering materials, they encourage you to make inferences, engage in the exchange of ideas, and sometimes struggle with material.

b. Study in manageable blocks. Some experts suggest 90 minutes, but I say do what works for you as long as you get the study time in.

25. Your room is probably not the best place to study.

    a. Going to a particular physical location to study conditions your brain to go into studying mode.

    b. Find a consistent place outside your room to study, perhaps the study lounge in the dorm or a floor in the library where studying actually happens.

26. Every single grade counts so don't miss an opportunity to earn the best course grade possible. A zero does much more damage than a low grade.

    a. A single zero can make or break your grade. For example, suppose you are a pretty good student with 10 assignments, 9 of which you earn an 85 and forget to turn in one. That one zero will result in an average of 76.5 On a ten point scale, your solid B becomes a solid C. Suppose you typically earn As and have 9 assignments on which you earn a 90. That one zero brings your average down from a 90 to an 81, again an entire letter grade. This particular example is overly simplistic, but you get the point. Turning in every single assignment, even if it's less than your best can avoid a significant negative impact on your grade.

b. Submit every single assignment. No matter what. If there are extenuating circumstances that will cause you to submit it late, speak with your instructor (before the due date) and accept the late penalty as opposed to a zero.

27. The day an assignment is due is not a good time to ask for an extension.

a. When you first get to college, you will (understandably) rely on tactics that worked well for you in high school. You may also find yourself so distracted by all the other goings on at your campus, that you do not realize an assignment is due until the last minute.

b. Begin each assignment the day it is assigned, especially bigger papers and projects. At the very least, review it so you know your instructor's expectations and won't get caught off guard by how much time you need to invest in it.

28. Sometimes you may disagree with a grade. Sometimes that issue may be resolved, but only if you do it right.

a. Your instructors and TAs are human, and sometimes grading can be subjective. Remember, the level and quality of work you submit as a college student is higher than what was expected of you in high school.

b. If you have an issue with an assignment/final grade, talk to your instructor about it. Be ready to provide evidence that your work is better than the grade reflects. "All my high school papers got As," is not evidence or a valid argument, but pointing to where you satisfied the criteria outlined in a rubric or where points where wrongly deducted is. Take your dispute up the ladder if you're not satisfied with the outcome.

29. Your academic advisor is there to help schedule classes and plan your course of study based on your academic and professional interests.

a. Approximately 90% of students see their academic advisor during their first year. This is wonderful! When you go, be prepared to have a discussion with your advisor versus getting your registration code and letting them lead the conversation. Just like with orientation, check your plan of study and browse through the course catalog prior to your appointment. Be ready with the course numbers and sections of the classes you'd like to take. Have alternatives ready in the event that classes fill to capacity before your registration slot.

b. Go see your academic advisor at least twice per semester – once to check-in and once to plan for next registration period. If you develop a solid relationship with your advisor, you may also see them about summer/internship/volunteer opportunities in your field. Talk to you advisor about any concerns you have with your major – wanting to change majors, fulfilling course requirements, etc. Let them be your first point of contact when you have academic uncertainty.

Social and Emotional Wellness

Because being a good great student requires a lot more than good grades.

30. No one gets through college alone.

    a. Sense of belonging can come from peers, teachers or staff, family, social and academic groups, and living-and-learning groups. There is research documenting a decline in GPA when students have a low sense of belonging. Whether you do or do not stay connected to people at home who can support you through this adjustment, it is also important to create connections on your campus as well.

    b. Create a support system. There may be people that you know from high school. They are usually a great place to start. Don't discount meeting new people. Whether it's someone in your dorm, 10 o'clock class, or professional organization, meet someone new. It may be for academic or social purposes. Make a goal of meeting a certain number of people each week (or month). If you're not extremely social, it may be a stretch, but you can always ask a class-related question to get you started.

31. You need 7-9 hours of sleep EVERY NIGHT for both your brain and your growing body.

    a. Your brain commits new information

to long-term memory during rapid eye movement cycle (REM), after about 6 – 8 hours of sleep. Therefore, studying smartly and getting a full night's sleep does more for your retention than pulling an all-nighter. Students with more stable sleep schedules have also been found to earn higher grades than those who do not (Allen Gomes, 2011). In addition, your brain cells refresh and clear out all the junk that can slow brain functions (The Sleep Doctor). Believe it or not, as a young adult, you also grow in your sleep.

b. Young adults between 18 – 25 are recommended to get 7 – 9 hours of sleep each night (National Sleep Foundation). While each individual's needs may vary, do your best to hit this range.

32. Frequent all-nighters are not a good idea.

a. Lack of sleep has physical and emotional consequences. Sleep deprivation – as little as an hour a night over time – can disrupt the brain's ability to consolidate and retain information and potentially affect future learning.

b. Young adult brains need sleep. See # 31.

33. It is important to find an outlet – intramural sports, gaming, a recreational team – that will add balance to your life and allow you to get your mind off of your issues and/or work out your frustrations.

    a. In 2017, more than half of students seeking campus counseling reported anxiety (61%) and a little less than half reported depression (49%) and stress (45%) (APA). There are so many life changes happening in college that it is important to develop coping mechanisms and methods for getting away from your issues and sometimes out of your own head – even if temporarily.

    b. Adjusting to college can be stressful, whether you realize it or not. Find an activity you enjoy that will take your mind off of any academic (or personal) issues and make that part of your regular routine.

34. Mental health is just as important as physical health. (Use the counseling center on campus.)

    a. Mental illness is common in the United States and can be treated. The key is diagnosis and seeking help. Many disorders begin to present themselves during childhood and adolescence which means there may already be a diagnosis by the time you get to college. Others may first appear during late adolescence and early 20s. The sometimes stressful and anxiety-inducing environment of college can be a trigger for some students. Whether it's anxiety, depression, manic-depressive (bipolar) disorder, or another issue, there are treatments that can help you take control of your situation. Experiencing triggers in college is common and can be properly addressed by a trained mental health professional. Counseling, like many other services on your campus are a resource covered by your student fees. There will be at least one session for which there will be no cost. Ongoing sessions will vary in cost from campus to campus.

b. If you feel confused, off-kilter, or not like yourself in any way, go to the counseling center on your campus. Don't shy away from talking to someone who is trained to help students think through their situations. Seeing a counselor can be a healthy thing and counselors are trained to listen objectively. They do not make decisions for you, but help you identify what is causing stress, anxiety, depression, etc. and address it in a helpful, healthy way.

35. Your food and dietary choices can work in your favor . . . or not.

   a. While most freshmen students do not gain 15 pounds, there is some weight gain among college freshmen (2.7 – 7.5 lbs., depending on the study). High school athletes who do not play in college sports are more prone to weight gain as their lifestyle becomes less active and more sedentary. The key is to be conscious of your food choices and whether or not there is structure in your eating habits.

   b. Make an attempt to eat on a regular schedule, balance your diet, and incorporate some level of physical activity. If you aren't sure how to make it work with your new life, check with student health for workshops. It also helps to keep (healthy) snacks in your room and bag to prevent hunger at inconvenient times.

36. Staying healthy can be a challenge as you're adjusting to college. Students often get sick because of stress, lack of sleep, and other poor habits.

a. The same way kindergarteners get sick easily, so do college students. Whether it's poor sleeping and eating habits – both of which can compromise your immune system – or living in close quarters, the college environment creates opportunities for you to get sick (LiveStrong).

b. Go to student health if you don't feel well. There is at least one visit per semester covered by your tuition. Check your student handbook or student health website to determine how often you can go based on your (parents') insurance plan.

More General College Things

Circling back to general college life. The icing on the cake ... networking, recommendation letters, student involvement ... things like that.

37. Events in your college/department are opportunities to meet faculty and administrators.

   a. Acquiring social capital – social relationships that result in a desired career and/or professional outcome (Parks-Yancy, 2012) – is a beneficial by-product of university enrollment. Each semester, there are different events, which on the surface may seem unnecessary and just another thing, that are actually an opportunity for you to invest in your college success in ways that are not directly connected to your academic performance. Creating social capital by developing relationships with faculty, staff, and administrators means you have a better chance of achieving many of your academic and career goals. The strength of your relationships, or lack thereof, can impact your access to different resources and knowledge of academic and career opportunities that are available. Get to know people in your college, not solely for self-serving reasons, but to expand your understanding of how the academic and professional systems on your campus work.

b. Your college or department will have often have meet-and-greets early in the fall semester. There will also be guest lectures/talks each semester as well. Attend at least one event each semester and make a point to meet a faculty or staff member. It can be an advisor, professor, assistant dean, or dean. Just meet someone to begin networking and creating relationships with the adults who will be part of your life for the next 4+ years.

38. College instructors typically operate differently than your high school teachers and need more lead time to write recommendation letters.

a. In high school, your teachers knew you well as they saw you every weekday and could probably run off a list of your positive attributes in very little time. Your college instructor, on the other hand, may see you 2-3 times a week (often in a larger class/lecture) and may know very little about you other than your grade and attendance record.

b. Ask for recommendation letters well in advance of due dates. (More tips in Appendix E.)

39. College ready communication can make or break whether you are taken seriously and/or receive a response.

   a. When you get to college, you may find that it is easier, or necessary, to email faculty and staff when you can't catch them in person. Understand that until someone gets to know you, this written correspondence is all they know of you. For this reason, it is paramount that your email be well written. Not necessarily APA or MLA style, but well. Use proper salutations, grammar, and punctuation. If you aren't certain whether or not an instructor has a degree, address them as "Dr. Such-and-such" and let them correct you in their reply. For everyone else, use "Ms." or "Mr.", also letting them give permission to use their first name based on their response. Also, be succinct. If there is a larger issue that needs discussion, ask when you can stop by their office to discuss the matter further.

   b. Write emails to faculty and staff in proper format, not like a text message. Re-read before sending, particularly if you write it while in your feelings about a specific issue.

40. Recommenders want to know you appreciate their endorsement of you and to know what happens next.

    a. Although some recommenders write (forms) letters and aren't interested in how the situation plays out, recommenders who know you and think well enough of you to vouch for you in a letter want to know if you got the thing you applied for.

    b. Immediately write a thank you email when someone writes a recommendation letter on your behalf. Also keep your recommender posted as to whether or not you receive the position, scholarship, etc.

41. College is a place to explore new things and grow. Expand your horizons and world view by taking advantage of what's offered on campus.

    a. Openness and curiosity rear their heads again on this one. Regardless of the type of institution you attend (2 yr. vs 4-year, public or private, co-ed or same sex, HBCU or PWI) you will meet people who are different than you and have different world views. There may be people who externally look like you and can't relate to your experiences while people you would never suspect have the same opinions on the cultural relevance and intellectual value of your favorite reality show. Be open to new experiences, new people, and new perspectives (Sullivan, 2012).

b. Go to seminars, lectures, and events that aren't for extra credit or participation points. Meet a new set of people and/or someone with a differing point of view. As you become (or plan to become) more familiar with college life in general and your campus specifically, attend a talk or meeting that is a little outside of your regular interests. Not really the outdoor type? Go out with the hiking club. Not really knowledgeable about a certain na-tional/cultural group? Attend a function to learn about traditions and history. Do something to expand your mind.

42. Your university, special programs, and stu-dent groups will typically (initially) send all communication to your school email only.

a. At one of my previous institutions, new students received as many as 30 emails per day. While it may be a lot to sift through and feel a little overwhelming, there is vital information delivered to your inbox every day. Deadlines. Important dates. Submission instructions. Homework tips. Take the time to check your email regularly because everything can't be captured in 280 characters or less.

b. Check your school email. EVERY DAY.

43. Community service/Service learning/Civic engagement is a great way to get your mind off of your own issues while giving back.

a. In addition to being a great thing to do, community service is now a graduation requirement for some colleges and universities. Some universities have offices of civic engagement and/or service learning programs. Those offices will provide service transcripts that can be submitted with your academic transcript for graduate school and/or employment. Some professional positions may expect it, and some fraternities/sororities also require it.

b. Seek out a service activity or organization that fits your interests and join it. Don't go overboard, though. The idea is to contribute to a cause greater than your-self for a few hours each week, not to cre-ate a personal challenge to do everything but homework.

44. During freshman year, limit your organiza-tions to two (2) – one related to your major and one for recreational purposes.

a. #30 mentioned creating a support sys-tem and #33 is about finding an outlet. Both things are important in concert with, not at the expense of, your academ-ic life. There is time for work, study, and play in a well-planned schedule. Be the student who works to balance the vari-ous aspects of their college life.

b. Time management is one of the biggest issues college faculty and staff see with first year students. While you do need an outlet, you also need to first manage your schedule. Don't fill it with so many things early in the semester because work feels easy. You will need to spend more time studying when classes get serious and it's easier to balance all your activities when there aren't too many.

45. Missing class in college is different than in high school. Excused absences are deter-mined differently.

a. The conditions under which you can get a written excuse for missing class are different/higher in college and going to student health won't cut it. Your parents cannot write you a note for being late or absent.

b. Don't go to class sick, but be ready to take the hit if you receive an unexcused absence. As long as you're going to every other class meeting, one or two absences won't significantly impact your performance. It is your responsibility to get the information you missed from your peers (or online platform) and because this is college, your instructors aren't obligated to get you up to speed. Do your best to schedule medical and dental visits outside of class time.

46. Loans MUST be paid back., Scholarships and grants do not.

a. In 2012, 71% of students graduating from college had student loan debt (Student Loan Hero). There are approximately 44.2M Americans with student loan debt, and as of 2018, the average is $39,400.

b. Think carefully when you accept each part of your financial aid package. Accept as many scholarships, grants, and work study as possible. If you are uncertain about the specifics of each award in your package, make an appointment with your financial aid office and sit down with a counselor.

47. Each summer should be spent on a research program, summer internship, or career-related volunteer opportunity.

    a. The summer after high school graduation was your last "free" summer. Going forward, each summer should be spent moving you in the direction of your future career. Even if you aren't certain what you want to do, there are still ways to productively use the summer. Volunteer positions help develop interpersonal, communication, and leadership skills that transfer to almost any industry. There are always ways to better prepare yourself for post-graduate work/study.

    b. In late October/early November begin searching for summer opportunities. Leave no stone unturned and apply early. If you are allowed to apply for a position toward the end of your first semester, DO IT. At that point you have no GPA, which could actually work in your favor. If you have to wait until the grades from fall semester are posted, apply during the winter break. I cannot tell you how many times applying early has worked in a student's favor. You may need recommendations from your instructors, so be certain to establish those relationships. Use the career center, support programs, and university staff with whom you've connected to get the skinny on summer opportunities. You can also get leads by following companies of interest on LinkedIn.

48. The career center (and department office) is a place to identify summer opportunities and sometimes part-time employment.

   a. In my administration positions, I've been approached by programs and companies/agencies that are looking for student researchers and summer employees. More often than you would believe, positions go unfilled because students do not apply. Sometimes it's because they do not meet the criteria, but it may also be because they do not see the direct correlation between a particular organization and their career aspirations. In response, I say apply anyway. Criteria are not always set in stone and there are transferrable skills you can acquire from work (and research) experiences that aren't obvious. The positions that go unfilled are often what we call "low-hanging fruit." Sometimes all you have to do is apply.

b. Locate the career center on campus, register (if necessary) and use it. Attend professional development workshops. Apply for programs and jobs that are recommended to you after doing a little research to determine the entire range of products or services they offer. For example, if you are on a pre-medical track, a position with the USDA may not seem relevant, but you could potentially gain experiences there that will relate to the biology and chemistry classes you will take.

49. The summers can also be used to get on track with missed credits (full courses) and/or retake a course to get your GPA on track (D or lower).

a. The majority of internships and summer (research) programs require a GPA of 3.0 or higher. However, there are select employers that may hire students with a 2.8 or better (NC A&T State University Office of Career Services, 2018). Check with the career center at your institution to verify the eligibility criteria for students in your major.

b. If your grades are less than stellar, use the summer to attend summer school and repair your GPA. If you live in another area, talk to your advisor about the pros and cons of taking courses at a different school to transfer credit (no grade) versus staying at your college and earning the grade.

50. Paying tuition entitles you to a good education, nothing more, nothing less.

a. College isn't cheap. And honestly, it isn't free. Whether your tuition is paid by you, your parents, scholarships and grant dollars, or loans, money is being spent for you to earn a quality education. Tuition increases approximately 2-3% each year (College Board) and for many young people, that price is making it more difficult to afford. Gone are the days of working a summer job (which usually pay minimum wage, by the way) to earn the next year's tuition. A full-time summer gig at today's minimum wage ($7.25, US Bureau of Labor Statistics) would earn a little less than $3500 <u>before taxes</u>. The average college tuition and fees (this doesn't include room and board) is approximately $10,000 per semester for in-state students at a public institution. In other words, you are paying for the education you either do or don't choose to get.

b. Demand the best education you can receive by actively participating in the process. This means going to class, participating in discussions, completing assignments, etc. For the things that you aren't certain how to do – talk to instructors, use help rooms, use other resources – ask for help. There is no shame in wanting to get the biggest bang for your buck.

BONUS:

51. Know you are capable of being a great college student and that putting in **your best effort** is all anyone asks of you.

    a. Every fall, millions of students begin their college careers and this year, you are included in that count. You are committing to get an education that will help you advance your personal, academic, and professional goals. It is exciting, but it can also be overwhelming at the same time.

    b. Take each day as it comes, being ambitious but realistic, and give it your all. Do all that you can do and when in doubt, ask. RAs, TAs, peer tutors, peer mentors, faculty, support staff, and administrators are all there for **you**.

About the Author

Dedra Eatmon, Ph.D. is founder and college transition strategist at Tassel to Tassel. Dr. Dee (as she is affectionately called by family and friends) is an engineer by trade and educator at heart. Dr. Dee began her career as a software engineer and, after transitioning to education has been both a teacher and an academic support program administrator.

She was responsible for software coding and development as a software systems engineer. As an eduator, Dr. Dee has experience in both high school and college teaching courses in mathematics, computer science, engineering, reasoning, and academic suc-cess. *College Ready 101: A field guide to a successful freshman year*, is her first book.

Dr. Eatmon is a graduate of North Carolina Agricultural & Technical State University, North Carolina State University, and the University of North Carolina at Chapel Hill. She currently resides in her hometown of Greensboro, NC where she teaches high school and teaches strategies for college success.

Appendices

A. Note taking methods

Depending on what type of learner you are, the note-taking method that works best for you may differ. There are several popular ones, five of which (along with their pros and cons) are covered in this *Medium* article:

https://medium.goodnotes.com/the-best-note-taking-methods-for-college-students-451f412e264e

A few others are covered here: https://www.oxfordlearning.com/5-effective-note-taking-methods/

B. Starter conversation with your professor

a. Ideally, you will meet your professor early in the semester when things are lukewarm and you have nothing in particular to discuss. That conversation goes like this:

Hi Dr. Such-and-Such. My name is Johnny and I am a freshman engineering major. I've not taken this class before and I want to make sure I'm successful in calculus. Are there any tips you have for me as a first-year student?

b. If, by some chance, you are meeting your instructor later in the semester and/or your grade isn't the best, try this:

Hi Dr. <u>Such-and-such</u>. My name is <u>Johnny</u> and I am a freshman <u>engineering</u> major. I'm experiencing a little difficulty in class and would like to review some of the information/concepts with you. [Note: If it's not office hours, add "Do you have time now, or should I come back during office hours?"]

C. Specific questions for office hours

As mentioned in the office hours item, going to your professor (or TA/tutor) and saying "I don't understand any of this" won't get you what you need. While it may be true, any of this is vague and does not indicate where you are experiencing difficulty. Rather than lay it all out in that manner, you can use any one of these approaches:

I am not sure I understand <u>insert topic here</u>. I understand it to be . . . . Am I on the right track?

I thought I knew how to do problem #x, but when I attempted it, I got stuck here.

I finished problem #x, but my answer doesn't match the back of the book/solution manual. Can you help me figure out where I messed up?

D. General office hours conversation

If you are having difficulty with a particular concept or homework problem, the items from Appendix C are helpful. However, if you feel you're on track and you still want to establish a relationship with your instructor, here are some things you can discuss:

Ask to clarify the concept being taught by sharing your understanding of it and then listen closely to what your instructor adds to it.

Go to get feedback on an assignment, quiz or test where you did not earn the grade you wanted. This is particularly helpful if solutions were not shared in class.

Share with them your study guide for the next test or and get their input on whether or not it's comprehensive enough.

E. Recommendation letter request tips

Requesting a letter of recommendation of a college instructor is a little different than requesting one from a high school teacher. College instructors prefer much more lead time and may not know you as well as your high school teachers, so you have to provide them with a little more info. In that same vein, make sure you request a recommendation from someone who actually knows you. College classes can be large and if all a professor can definitively write in their letter is your course grade and attendance, that won't be very helpful. Creating relationships is important. That's why I encourage you to visit your instructors early and visit them often.

When possible, ask in person, especially the first time you make the request of someone. This added touch may determine whether your request is honored.

Be prepared to provide your recommender with your resume, a list of your activities, (a link to) the description of to what you're applying, the submission link (or addressed envelope, if on paper) for the recommendation to be submitted, any essay you are writing for the job/program/organization, and maybe a small blurb about why you are interested in this particular program/school/job/etc.

References

The Sleep Doctor
https://www.thesleepdoctor.com/2017/03/30/teens-need-sleep-think/

National Sleep Foundation
https://sleepfoundation.org/excessivesleepiness/content/how-much-sleep-do-we-really-need-0

National Library of Medicine, NIH (sleep)
https://www.ncbi.nlm.nih.gov/pmc/articles/PMC4180265/

American Psychological Association
http://www.apa.org/monitor/2017/09/numbers.aspx

Student Loan Hero
https://studentloanhero.com/student-loan-debt-statistics/

College Board
https://trends.collegeboard.org/college-pricing/figures-tables/average-rates-growth-published-charges-decade

Psychology Today
https://www.psychologytoday.com/us/blog/the-gravity-weight/201309/college-weight-gain-debunking-the-myth-the-freshman-15

LiveStrong
https://www.livestrong.com/article/209706-the-reasons-college-kids-get-sick/

Allen Gomes, A., Tavares, J., & de Azevedo, M. H. P., 2011. Sleep and academic performance in undergraduates: A multi-measure, multi-predictor, approach. Chronobiology International, 28(9), 786-801.

Conley, D. T., (2008). Rethinking college readiness. New Directions in Higher Education, 144, 3 – 13.

Cowser Yancy, D. C, Sutton-Haywood, M., Hermitte, E., Worthy Dawkins, P., Rainey, K., & Parker, F. E., 2008. The impact of the freshman academy/learning communities on student progression and engagement. The Journal of Negro Education, 77(3), 250 – 263.

Dweck, C., 2006. *Mindset: The new psychology of success.* Ballantine Books.

Giner, S. A., Kelly-Reid, J. E., & Mann, F. B., 2017. Graduation rates for selected cohorts 2008 – 12; Outcome measure for Cohort Year 2008; Student financial aid, academic year 2015 – 16; and admissions in postsecondary institutions, Fall 2016. NCES Report.

Knowlden, A. P., Sharma, M., Bernard, A. L., 2012. Sleep hygiene of a sample of undergraduate students at a midwestern university. American Journal of Health Studies, 27 (1), 23 – 32.

Mueller, P. A., and Oppenheimer, D. M. (2014). The pen is mightier than the keyboard: Advantages of longhand over laptop note taking. Psychological Science, 25(6), 1159 – 1168.

Sullivan, P., 2012. Essential habits of mind for college readiness. College English, 74 (6), 547 – 553.

Made in the USA
Middletown, DE
16 February 2019